MW01491608

Journal

Belle P. Brewer

Made in the USA
Monee, IL
26 April 2022

95419898R00057